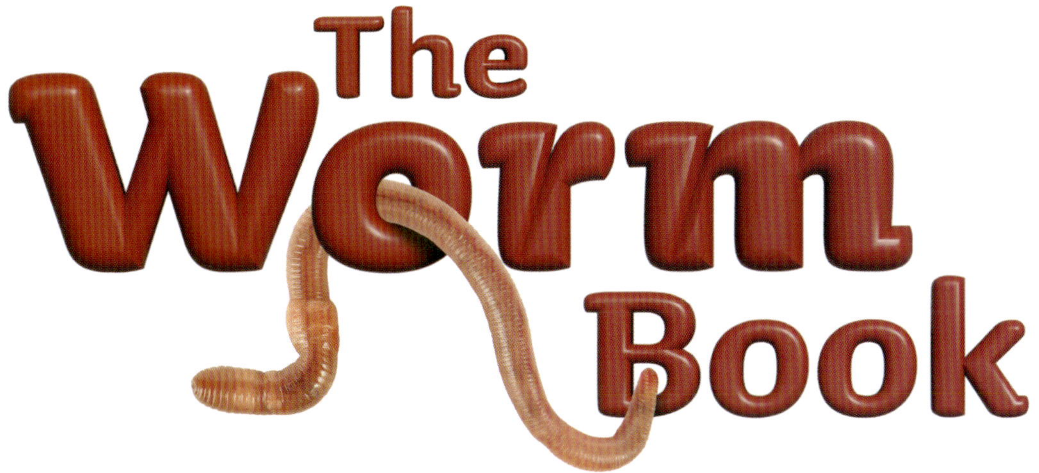

Nature's Recycler

Karen Tayleur
& Guy Holt

First published in 2024 by
wild dog
wdog.com.au
Melbourne, Australia

Designed by Guy Holt
Illustrations by Guy Holt

ISBN: 9781742036694 (hbk)
Printed and bound by Everbest Printing Co Ltd

10 9 8 7 6 5 4 3 2 1   24 25 26 27 28

Front cover SomprasongWittayanupakorn, Richard Peterson; title page Richard Peterson; imprint page hsagencia; page 2 Todorean-Gabriel, Rattiya Thongdumhyu; page 3 littlesam, schankz; page 4–5 Richard Peterson; page 6 Guy Holt; page 7 Eric Isselee, Jaewcams, IrinaK; page 8 neenawat khenyothaa; page 9 Andriy R, Torsten Rempt; page 10 golf bress; page 11 Inna Horosheva, Katherine Wallis, MilanTomazin; page 12 kukurund; page 13 Debra Angel, kukurund; page 14 Norjipin Saidi; page 15 EreborMountain, Vladislav Sagaidik; page 16 Kateryna Kon; page 17 blue-sea.cz, Ernie Cooper; page 18 Gerald Robert Fischer, Jack Pokoj; page 19 zdenek_macat; page 20 hsagenica, Matt Benoit, Ruslan Kerimov; page 21 Andrei Kuzmik, schankz, Super Prin, Valentina Razumova; page 22 Jay Ondreicka, Nora Yusuf, schankz; page 23 Dr Beverley Van Praagh, Pee Paew; page 24 Electric Egg; page 25 Guy Holt, m.malinika; page 27 Toeizuza Thailand; page 28 MichaelJayBerlin; back cover MakroBetz, schankz.

Contents

Introduction

What animal has no bones but can move, has no lungs but can breathe and has no eyes but can see? The remarkable worm.

Roundworm

A worm's diet consists of organic matter such as dead plants, fungi, bacteria and even dead animals. Worms digest this matter, absorb the remaining energy and then turn it into poo, known as worm **castings**. Worm castings are packed with nutrients that fertilise the soil to help feed new plants. They also bind soil particles to help reduce soil erosion and improve water retention. This is why these worms are known as nature's recyclers.

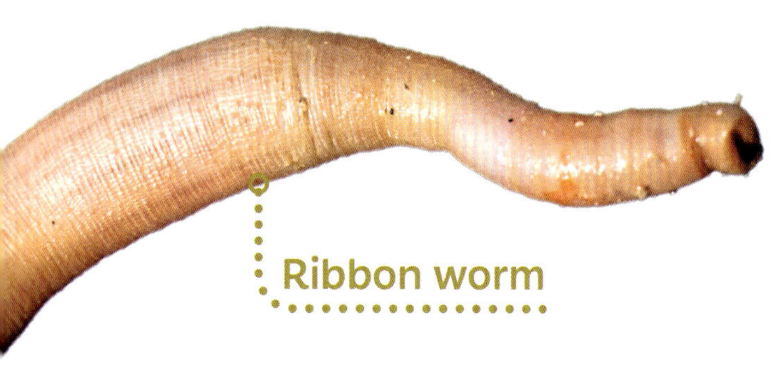

As well as recycling dead plants into nutrients for new plants, worms burrow through the earth, loosening and **oxygenating** the soil. This leaves space for water to drain from the surface, helping to soak up water and avoid floods. The tunnels worms make also create space for plants to root.

There are around 20,000 species of worm. The four major groups of worm include the segmented worm, the roundworm, the ribbon worm and the flatworm. The earthworms you can find in the garden are segmented worms.

Segmented worms (annelids)

There are around 6,000 species of segmented worm worldwide.

The worms you find in your garden are *Phylum annelida*, the earthworm.

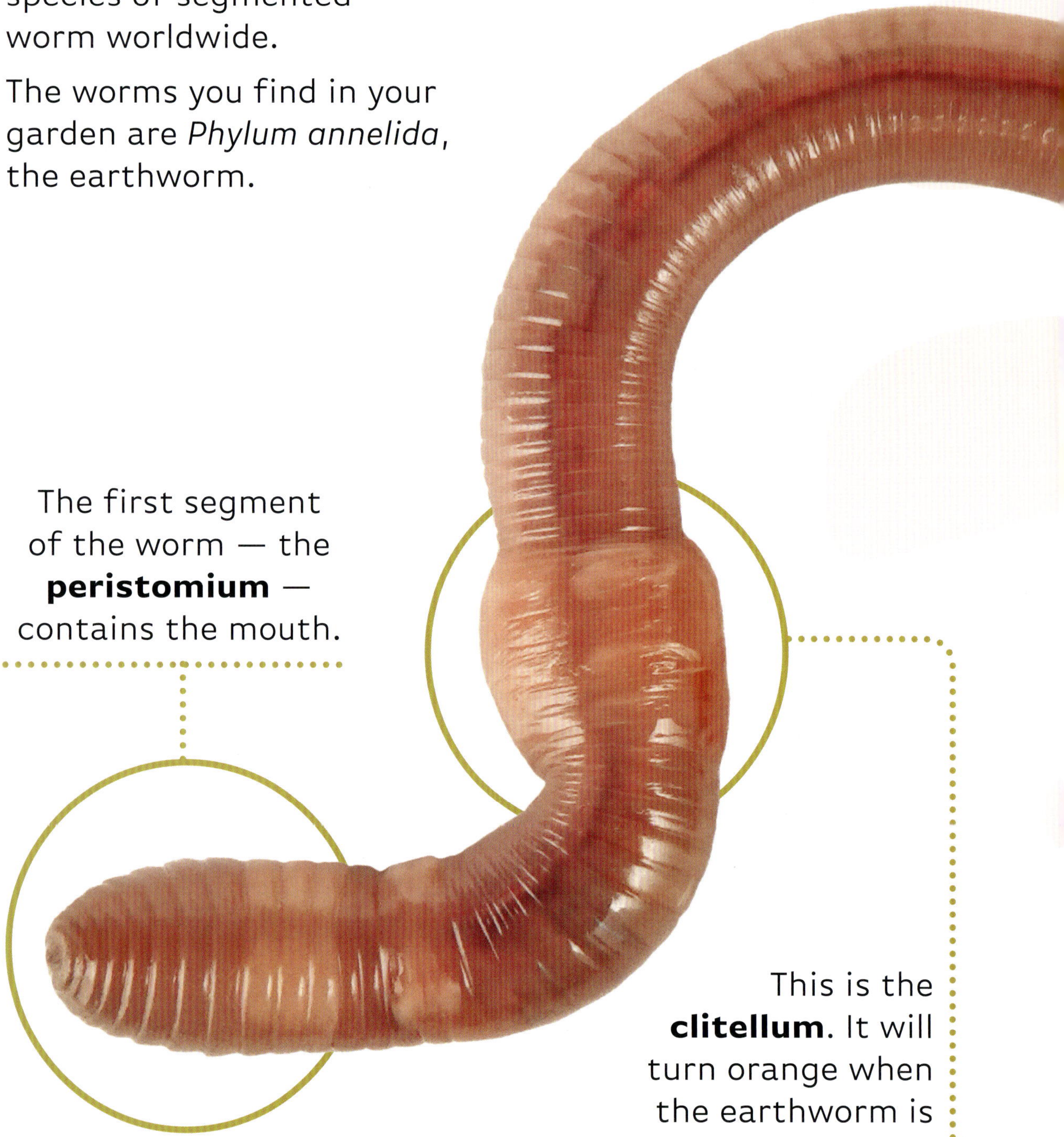

The first segment of the worm — the **peristomium** — contains the mouth.

This is the **clitellum**. It will turn orange when the earthworm is ready to mate.

An earthworm has no eyes. Instead, it has cells in its body called **receptors** that can sense light or darkness.

It has no ears, but it can sense the vibrations of movement through its body.

The earthworm has no nose but breathes by absorbing oxygen through its skin.

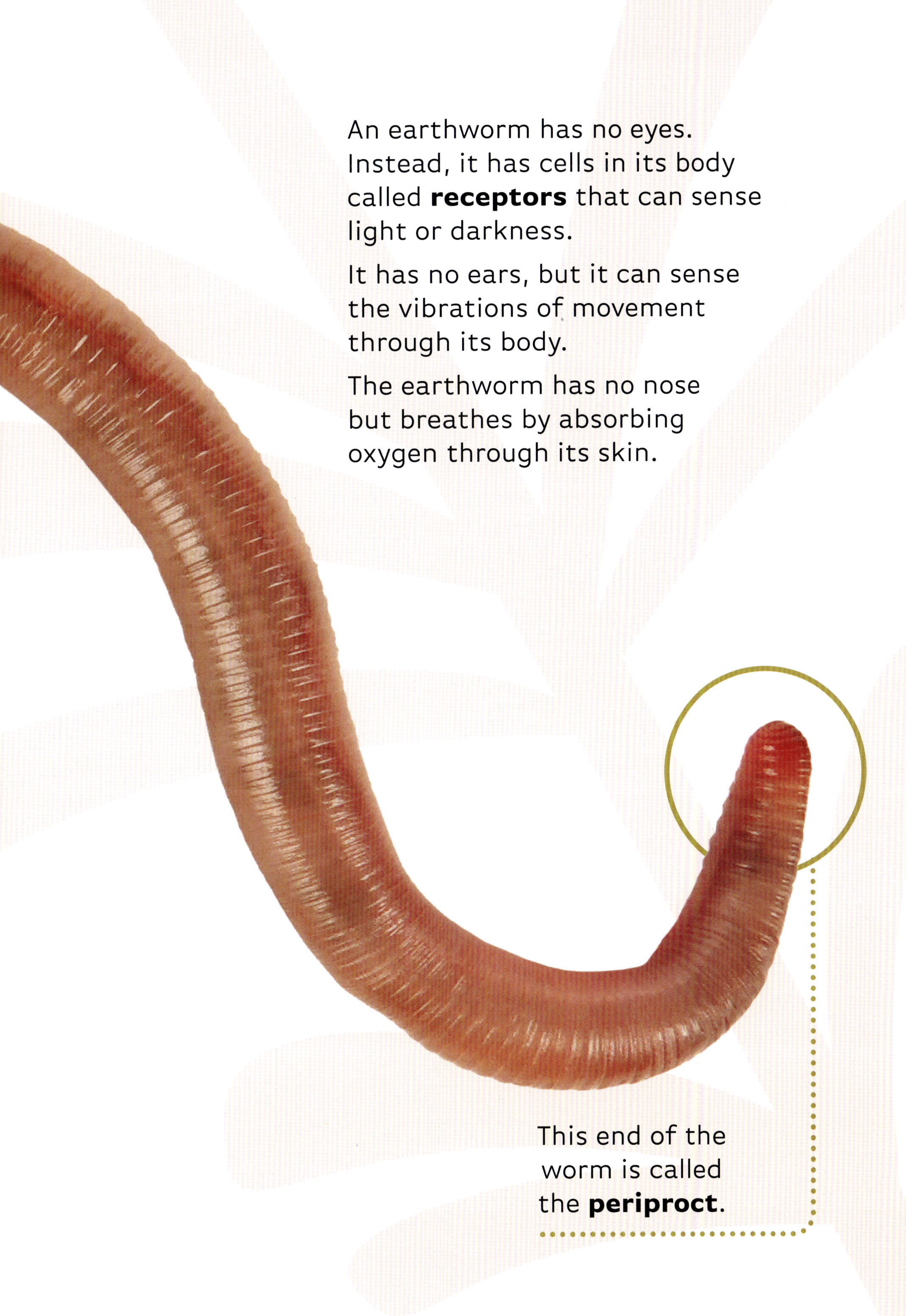

This end of the worm is called the **periproct**.

Instead of one heart, earthworms have an **aortic arch** made up of five arches that pump blood around the body.

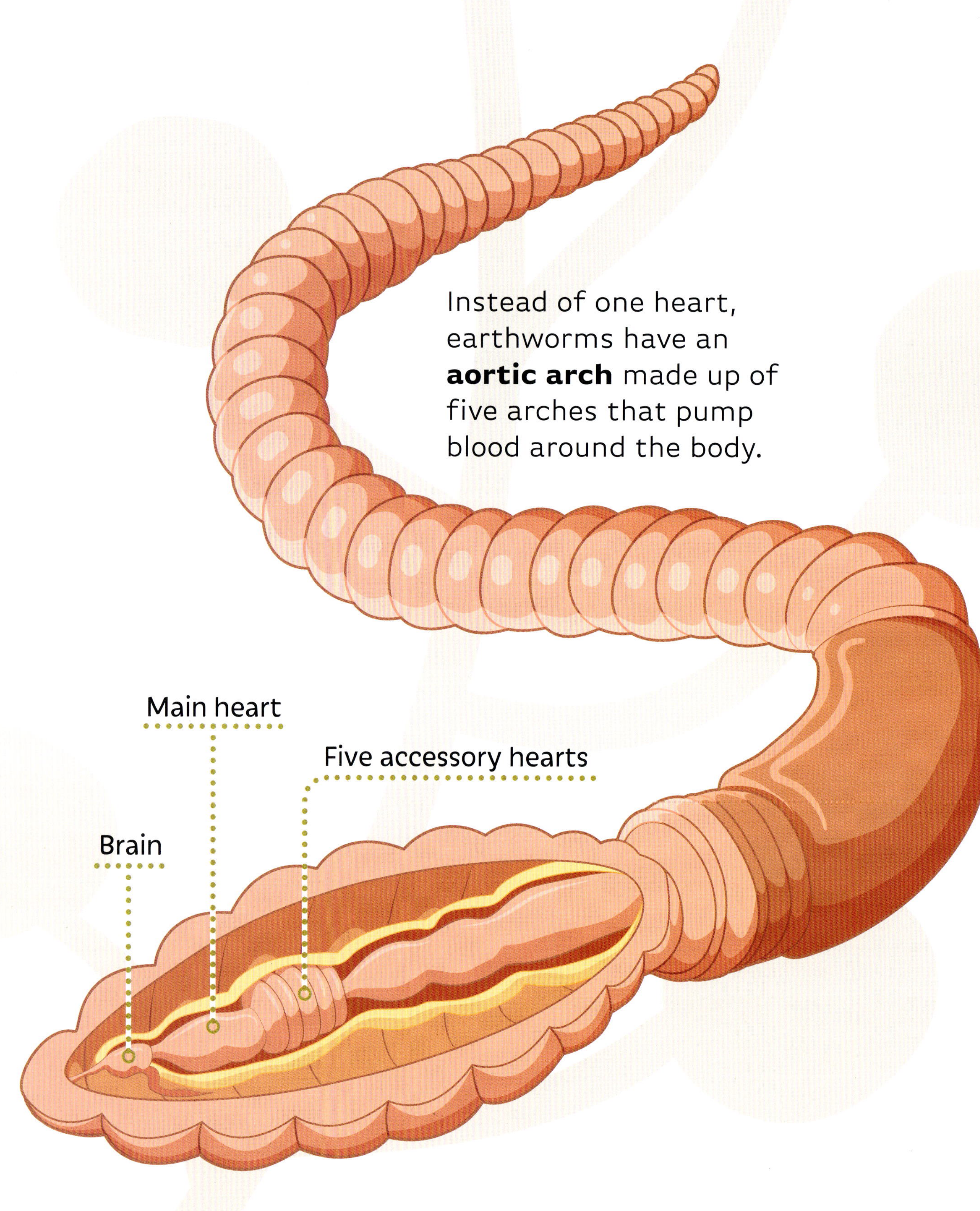

An earthworm has no legs or feet. To help it move it uses the muscles in its segments. Each segment of an earthworm's body is covered in tiny **setae**, or bristles. The worm stretches and contracts its muscles to move forward or backward over a surface. The setae grip the surface to keep the worm from slipping.

Predators are animals that hunt other animals for food. The natural predators of the earthworm include frogs, birds and lizards.

Worms don't eat living plants, but are happy to eat food scraps, dead plants or dead creatures.

Worms can eat their own body weight in food every day. When an earthworm eats organic matter, its castings help to fertilise the soil.

This is an earthworm poo tower!

Earthworms produce **cocoons**, which can contain as many as 20 eggs. It takes around 23 days for the worm to escape from their egg and eat the nourishing **albumen** in the cocoon. When they are big enough, they leave the cocoon to begin their life in the soil.

Unhatched earthworm egg.

Earthworm cocoons are around 3–4 millimetres long.

Worms are **hermaphrodites**, which means they have both male and female reproductive organs.

Oxygen is an essential ingredient for healthy underground **microbes** and those plant parts that live below the soil surface. Earthworms **oxygenate** the soil and help transport minerals and nutrients as they tunnel. These tunnels loosen and **aerate** the soil and improve soil drainage.

Earthworms produce mucus all over their bodies. This lubricant helps them move and binds the soil tunnels so they keep their shape. It also stops the worms from being covered in dirt.

Other segmented worms

Leeches are annelids, like the earthworm, but they live in wet places instead of underground. Leeches are **carnivorous**, and some are also **haematophagous**, which means they drink the blood of other animals.

The Christmas tree worm is a segmented worm with two 'crowns'. The worm pumps water over the crowns to filter out tiny plants and animals to snack on. These worms settle on stony coral and can live up to 30 years.

The feather duster worm is a marine segmented tubeworm with a crown of feathers that can measure up to 25 centimetres. The worm lives inside a long tube that it builds from sand and mud. The worm attaches to solid surfaces like rock or coral.

Ragworms, a type of annelid worm, are mainly marine creatures. They hide under rocks, in seaweed and burrow in wet sand or mudflats. The ragworm is a **scavenger**, feeding mainly on plankton, mud, and **detritus**, as well as a **predator**, preying on other soft-bodied animals.

This ragworm has long bristles on its segments that look like frills.

A ragworm peeking out of the sand showing its teeth.

Ribbon worms (proboscises)

Ribbon worms are one of the simplest animals to have a circulatory system and a gut that has a separate mouth and anus. Most species are less than 20 centimetres long, but a giant species of ribbon worm called the *Lineus longissimus* can reach up to 30 metres in length.

A ribbon worm enjoying an insect meal.

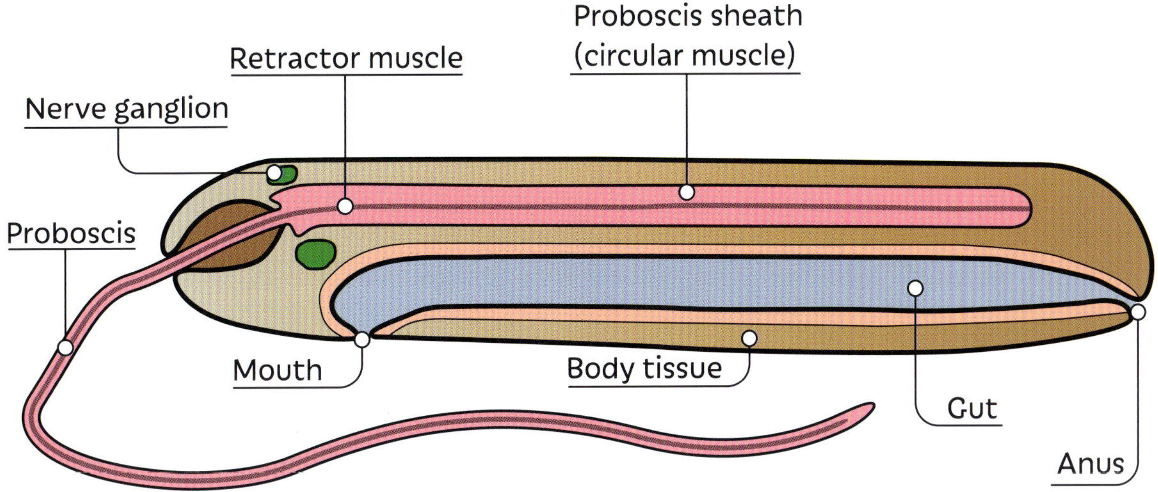

The ribbon worm has a long, tube-shaped organ called a **proboscis** that it pushes out of its body to catch its prey. Some proboscises have special spines at the end that pierce prey and inject toxins. The prey is then pulled towards the worm's mouth as the proboscis slides back into the worm's body.

Most ribbon worms are **aquatic** but some live on the land. They eat other worms, crustaceans and molluscs.

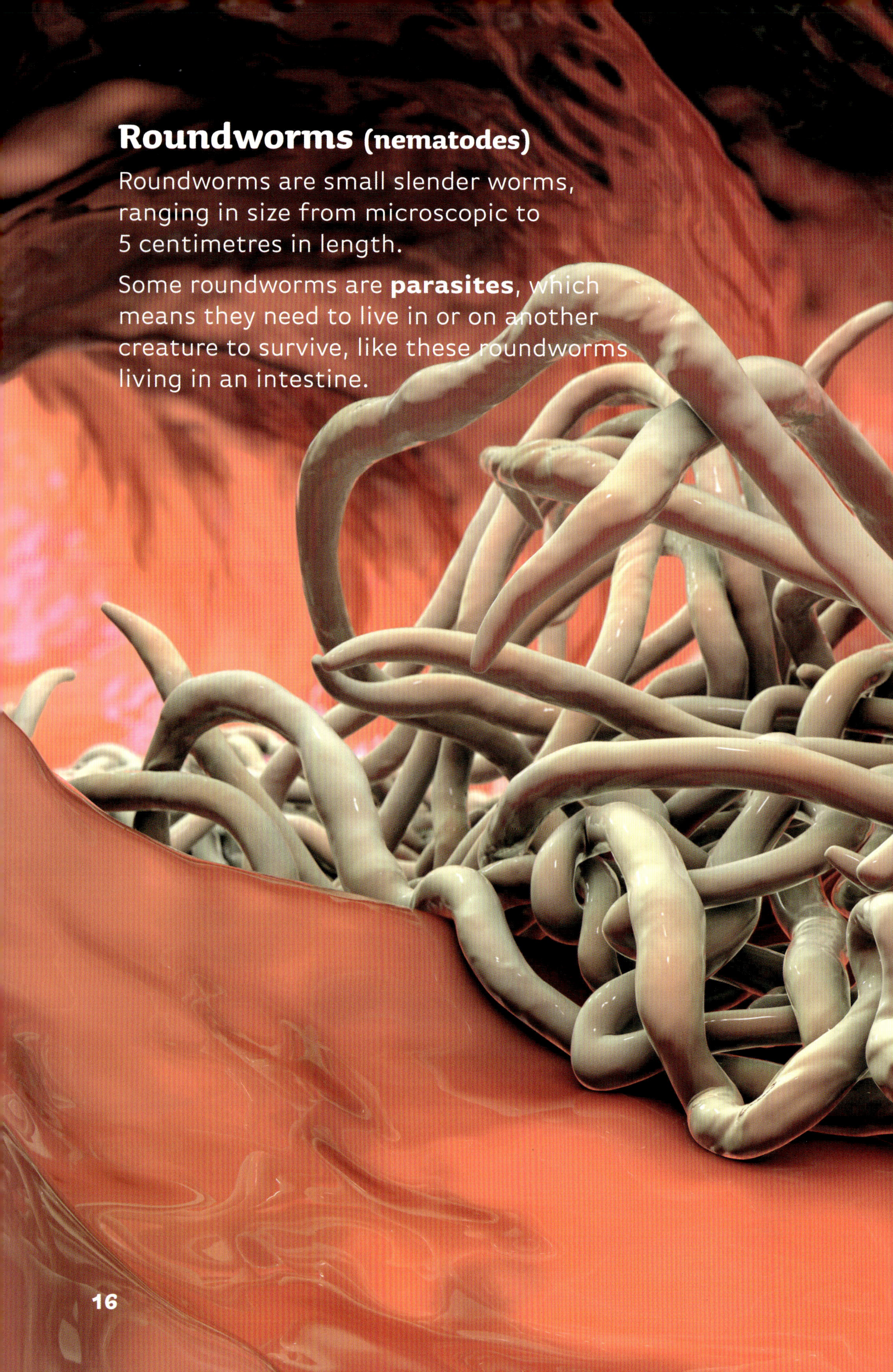

Roundworms (nematodes)

Roundworms are small slender worms, ranging in size from microscopic to 5 centimetres in length.

Some roundworms are **parasites**, which means they need to live in or on another creature to survive, like these roundworms living in an intestine.

Flatworms (platyhelminthes)

The bodies of flatworms are flat and unsegmented. Some flatworms like this blue racing stripe flatworm are free-living, which means they do not rely on other animals for survival. This worm lives in the ocean, on reefs, on coral and under rocks.

Flatworms prefer to feed on **invertebrates** that can't easily move, such as mussels.

Flatworms have two eyespots that help them sense light.

Marine flatworms are usually brightly coloured, which warns potential **predators** that they are toxic.

Flatworms have stem cells that can regenerate body parts. They can even grow a new head and brain.

A flatworm's mouth and throat (**pharynx**) are isolated in a single opening in its stomach. It uses this like a short vacuum cleaner hose to suck out the insides of its prey. It also uses the pharynx to push waste out of its body.

Flatworms have tiny hair-like growths (**cilia**) underneath their skin. The cilia are like oars, propelling the flatworm forward.

This broadhead land planarian flatworm lives in the tropical rainforest of Borneo. It is known as a hammerhead worm. The slimy covering on its body helps the worm to move and keeps it from drying out.

Land planarian flatworms are carnivorous and feed mainly at night. They eat slugs, small snails, and **protozoans**, which are a single-celled microorganisms.

Weird and wonderful

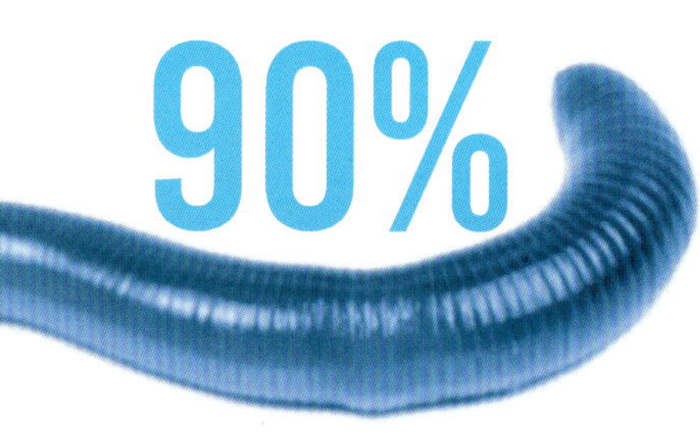

Around 70 per cent of the human body is made up of water, while worms are around 90 per cent water.

Charles Darwin must have really liked worms – he studied them for 38 years. He even wrote a book called *The Formation of Vegetable Mould Through the Action of Worms*. Darwin considered worms the most important creatures on Earth.

You can find worms on every continents on Earth, except for Antarctica.

The expression 'a can of worms' can be traced back to the 1950s in the USA when people could buy sealed metal cans of worms for fishing. Once opened, the worms would quickly escape unless the top was kept firmly closed.

If a worm is cut in half (or maybe pulled in half by a bird) it can grow new segments. This can happen only if the worm is cut right behind the clitella, which is near its head.

It would take around 2,000 worms to process the average daily food waste from a family of four.

Worms are light-sensitive. When worms detect light through their skin, they will move to a darker area to keep their skin moist. If they stay in the light for over an hour, they will become paralysed.

Worms and dinosaurs lived in the same period. While dinosaurs went extinct around 230 million years ago, worms are still with us!

The teredo worm or shipworm is found on Gumbaynggirr land in New South Wales. It is often consumed as bush tucker to treat general sickness. It looks like a long thin worm but is actually a shell-less saltwater mollusc.

A worm is an invertebrate animal, which means it has no backbone. Worms are cold-blooded and their bodies are made up of 90 per cent water. If the skin of the worm dries out, it will suffocate.

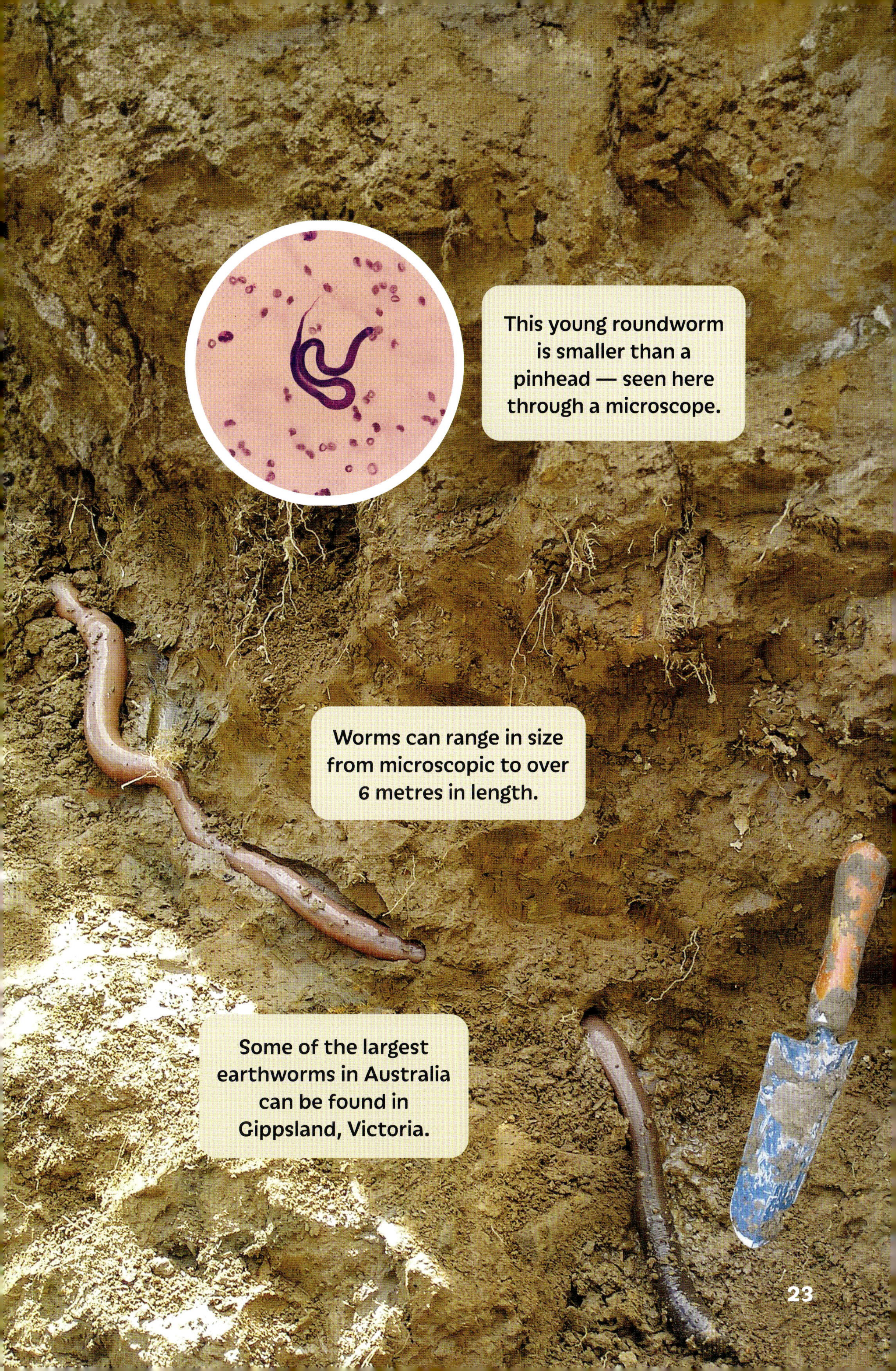
This young roundworm is smaller than a pinhead — seen here through a microscope.
Worms can range in size from microscopic to over 6 metres in length.
Some of the largest earthworms in Australia can be found in Gippsland, Victoria.

Composting

When you throw your food scraps into the bin, they may end up buried in landfill. Food waste buried under other rubbish leaves it without access to oxygen.

Anaerobic decomposition is bad for the environment. Methane is a significant contributor to the increasing amount of greenhouse gas trapped in Earth's atmosphere. The more greenhouse gas in the atmosphere, the hotter the planet gets.

Composting, however, is a fun and pollution-free way of breaking down food waste. When food scraps are composted, they have access to oxygen. This allows food waste to decompose without producing methane, as the methane-producing **microbes** are not active in the presence of oxygen. This is called **aerobic decomposition**.

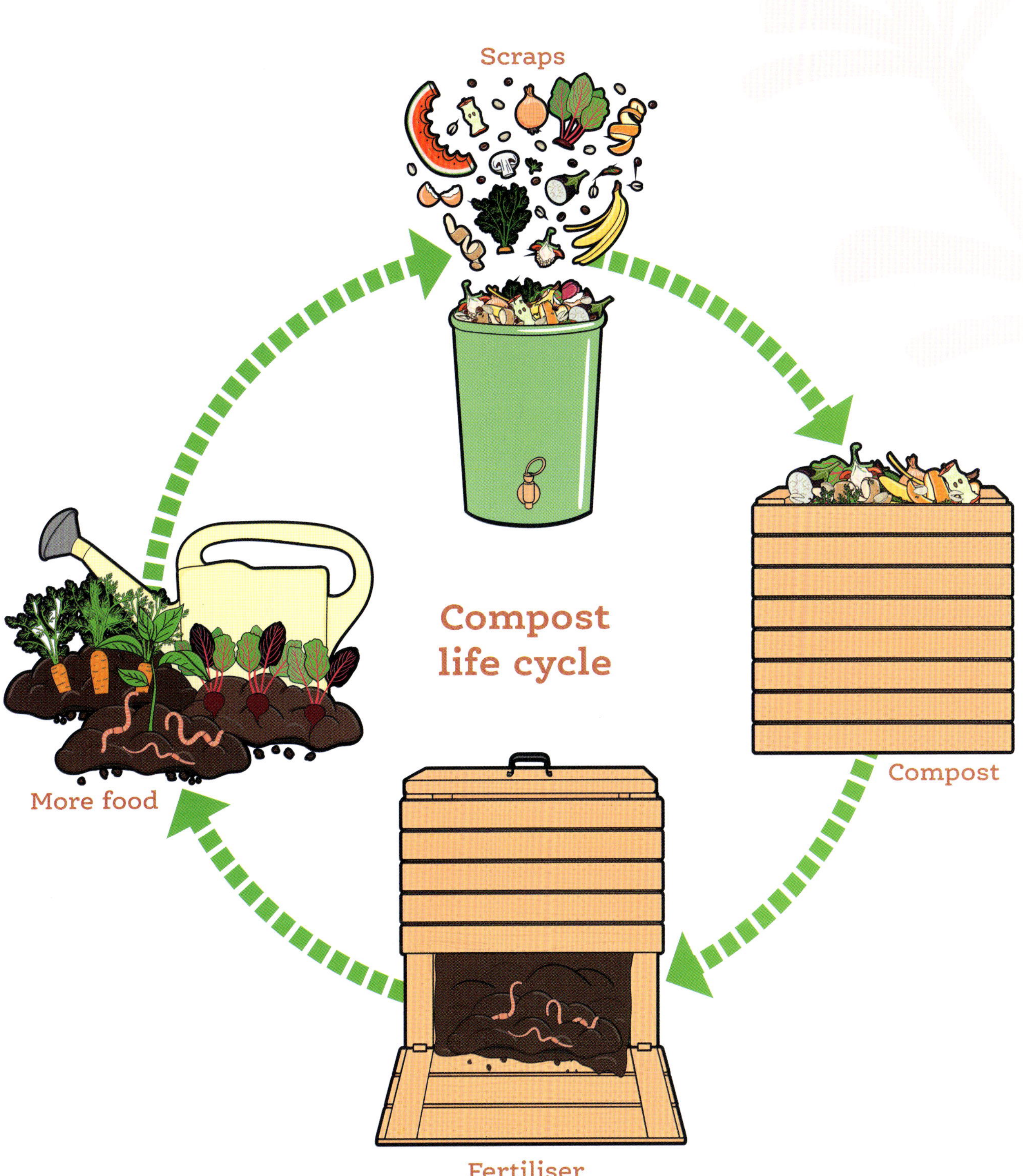

You can compost your food scraps at home, including coffee grinds, fruit and vegetable peelings. Food such as dairy, meat or grains should not be used as they will attract rodents.

You can put a small bin in your kitchen to easily empty your lunch box or dispose of other food scraps.

Make your own worm farm

Vermiculture is a kind of worm farming, where earthworms turn organic waste into rich castings called **vermicompost**. You can create your own worm farm in your garden or at school.

A wooden box is ideal for your worm farm, as it stops the compost from getting too wet. To set this farm up, fill the box with these layers:

First layer
This is your base layer and getting the mix right will ensure that air can circulate through your compost. Place materials like twigs, leaves, old potting mix and mulch.

Second layer
The next layer should contain lots of garden clippings and food scraps. You might also like to add some wet paper to help keep the compost from drying out.

Third layer
Finally, add a layer of soil to make sure the compost doesn't stink up your garden!

Around 200 earthworms should be placed inside the box.

Be sure to mix up, or aerate, your compost every week. You should also keep it covered up with a lid to keep the farm dark and moist for the worms.

Many people consider red earthworms to be the most suitable for worm farms. Red worms reproduce faster than regular earthworms and can double in numbers every three months. Red worms can eat half their body weight in food each day.

Make sure your farm isn't in full sun all day. While the worms in your farm can survive temperatures of between 4–26 degrees Celsius, they are happiest at temperatures between 10–21 degrees Celsius.

You can place pans underneath the worm farm to catch **leachate**, which is the liquid that passes through the compost. It is liquid fertiliser that can be added to your garden.

Vermiculture produces little to no odour at all. If your farm starts to smell, it might be a sign you need to aerate the compost pile more frequently.

After a few months of composting in your worm farm, you might notice the pile is dry and crumbly. This means it is ready to use as fertiliser for your garden.

Using fertiliser for your garden is like conditioning your hair. It helps your soil retain moisture, adding nutrients and gives it the ideal texture for plants to thrive.

Help nature's recyclers do their work and get composting!

Glossary

aerate – to supply or fill with air

aerobic decomposition – the breakdown of organic matter in the presence of oxygen

albumen – a water-soluble protein

anaerobic decomposition – the breakdown of organic matter in the absence of oxygen

annelid – a worm whose body is divided into segments, like rings joined together

aortic arch – a segment of the aorta artery that helps move blood around the body

aquatic – living or growing in water

castings – worm waste

carnivorous –feeding on the flesh of other animals

cilia – tiny hair-like structures

clitella/clitellum – a thickened region of skin in earthworms and leeches

cocoon –a covering made by animals to protect their young

compost – a mixture of various kinds of organic matter undergoing decay, used for fertilising land

detritus – loose material such as organic fragments (created by the disintegration of a creature) or rock particles

haematophagous – feeding on the blood of other animals

hermaphrodite – an animal that has both male and female reproductive organs

invertebrate – an animal without a backbone or bony skeleton

leachate – the liquid that drains from a worm farm or landfill

microbe – a microorganism, usually one of vegetable nature; a germ

oxygenate – to add oxygen

parasite – a plant, animal or fungus that lives on another living thing

periproct – the flexible area surrounding the anus

peristomium – the first body segment of an annelid worm

pharynx – throat

predator – an animal that kills and eats other animals

proboscis – a long, tube-shaped organ the ribbon worm pushes out of its body to catch prey

protozoan – an organism or living thing, belonging to a group of organisms called protists

receptors – a cell that receives light or heat and activates a nerve to send a message to the brain

setae – small bristles that cover an earthworm's body to help grip

scavenger – an animal that feeds on decaying or dead organic material

vermicompost – the product of organic material that has been processed by worms

vermiculture – worm farming

Index